DEAD DINOSAURS

DEAD DINOSAURS

MARTIN OLIVER

Illustrated by
Daniel Postgate

For Isabelle and Katie with love

Scholastic Children's Books,
Euston House, 24 Eversholt Street,
London, NW1 1DB, UK
A division of Scholastic Ltd
London ~ New York ~ Toronto ~ Sydney ~ Auckland
Mexico City ~ New Delhi ~ Hong Kong

Published in the UK by Scholastic Ltd, 2000

10 digit ISBN 0 590 19646 4
13 digit ISBN 978 0590 19646 8

Typeset by TW Typesetting, Midsomer Norton, Somerset
Printed and bound in Denmark by Nørhaven Paperback A/S, Viborg

17 19 20 18 16

CONTENTS

Introduction   7

In the beginning   11

Dinosaur times   24

Fabulous families   42

Fantastic fossils   51

Food, glorious food   65

Potty palaeontologists   84

Dinosaur detectives   106

Disappearing dinosaurs   124

Epilogue   132

INTRODUCTION

Dinosaurs are decidedly dead. In fact, you can't get much deader than dinosaurs – they've been extinct so long that they're even deader than dodos.

I'VE BEEN EXTINCT LONGER THAN YOU!

But even though dinosaurs died out millions of years ago, interest in them is still very much alive and kicking. So why *are* people still interested in them? After all, there's nothing as boring as yesterday's news!

There are plenty of reasons why people get bitten by the dinosaur bug. Some get hooked when they discover that dinosaurs came in the most amazing sizes. After all, at 6m high, Tyrannosaurus rex was the largest meat-eating animal ever to trample the earth, while at over 15m high when it raised its snakelike neck, the plant-eating Supersaurus could have looked through the window of a fifth storey building (if they'd existed at the time).

I'LL LICK YOUR WINDOWS CLEAN FOR A FIVER.

Another reason for dinomania is that they also came in the most incredible shapes. Try to imagine the weirdest-looking alien you can – then think of Triceratops. In a "Spot the Strangest Creature Competition", Triceratops would win hands, feet and triple horns down!

WIERDO!

Other people become dinosaur-crazy because they find a fossil, while yet others want to study dinosaurs and solve the greatest mystery of all – why they became extinct. Imagine the thrill of actually discovering a dinosaur – and that's just the beginning. Then there's the excitement of trying to fit the pieces together, working out what sort of dinosaur it was and how it lived.

With so much to learn about dinosaurs there's plenty of room for argument, and the people who argue about dinosaurs for a living are called palaeontologists (pally-ont-olo-gists) – the name given to anyone who studies fossils.

Palaeontologists are a mixture of explorer, scientist and detective, and while this may sound very exciting, some of the tongue-twisting, brain-straining words they use often aren't. Most palaeontologists are experts at both geology (the study of rocks where dinosaur fossils are found) and zoology (the study of the bones and behaviour of modern animals) – and sometimes you almost need an "ology" of your own to understand what they're on about...

OBSERVE THIS CLASSIC EXAMPLE OF A CARNIVEROUS QUADRUPED PANTHERA LEO OF THE FAMILY FELIDAE.

MEANING: THIS LION, BELONGING TO THE CAT FAMILY, IS A TYPICAL FOUR-LEGGED MEAT-EATER.

PANTHERA LEO DISPLAYS STALKING TECHNIQUES TYPICAL OF A PREDATORY ANIMAL WHEN SPOTTING ITS PREY. IT IGNORES A SMALL GRAZING HERBIVORE TO FOLLOW A BIPED FROM THE HOMO SAPIEN SPECIES.

MEANING: THE LION HUNTS BY STALKING ITS PREY. IT IGNORES A SMALL PLANT EATER TO FOLLOW A TWO-LEGGED HUMAN BEING.

However, so long as you're not put off by some of the longest words in the English language, you'll discover some of the longest, tallest and strangest animals that ever walked on the earth. Enter the mind-boggling world of dead dinosaurs and discover some of the most amazing animals that ever existed – a world of unsolved mysteries, of life, death and everything in between.

Be prepared to find out about dinosaur disasters, dinosaur diets and even rotten relics like dinosaur dung. Try to make your own mind up about whether dinosaurs were warm-blooded or if they were the predecessors of modern-day birds. You can put Tyrannosaurus rex on trial, be a dinosaur detective, test your friends with our dead dinosaur quizzes and be astonished by our dead amazing facts. Whatever you discover about dinosaurs it's sure to be dead interesting, dead exciting and dead cool – but one thing it will never be is deadly dull!

IN THE BEGINNING

The first dinosaur discovery

So how were the dinosaurs rediscovered? Who brought them back to life millions of years after their extinction? To discover the answers, we need to go back to the sleepy Sussex countryside of England in 1822.

King George IV was on the throne, and only nine years earlier the explorer Johann Burkhardt had sailed down the Nile to introduce Europe to the wonders of the Egyptian pharaohs. However, the peace and quiet of that spring day in 1822 was about to be shattered by the discovery of something even more amazing and far, far older. After 65 million years, the world of the dinosaurs was about to come to light...

Dr Gideon Mantell was preparing to make a call on a sick patient with his wife, Mary. The sun was shining down as the couple left their house in Lewes and made their way along the rough track to Cuckfield. Mary admired the view of the fields, but her husband seemed quiet and preoccupied.

"Are you thinking about the book?" she asked.

Dr Mantell nodded. *The Fossils of the South Downs* was his pride and joy. He'd always been fascinated by fossils, and

11

over the years he'd built up a large collection of them. It had long been his ambition to write a book about them, and he'd finally finished it. It had taken him longer than he'd expected, and it was just as well that Mary had been happy to help him prepare the illustrations for it.

"It had better do well," he thought to himself. He hadn't told Mary that he'd been spending so much time on his fossil collections that his practice was beginning to suffer. The doctor kept his worries to himself, and soon they found themselves outside the patient's house.

"Won't you come in with me?" Dr Mantell asked on the doorstep. "I shouldn't be too long."

Mary shook her head. "I think I'll go for a walk — it's a shame to be cooped up indoors during this weather. Don't worry, I'll be back soon."

She waved goodbye then headed off. Brisk steps took her out of the village, and once she was in the country, she took some deep breaths of fresh air. The hot sun slowed her pace, and she began humming a tune as she strolled on down the road. After a few

hundred metres, Mary turned a corner and found her way blocked by a group of workmen repairing the surface of the road. They smiled and stopped working for a few moments as she picked her way past them and the piles of stones heaped up by the roadside.

Mary was about to continue when something caught her eye. What was that? There was something unusual about some of the stones to her left. It was the way they caught the light – they were shiny and a strange shape.

"I'd better take a closer look," she thought, bending down to sort through them. "I'm sure these are fossils," she muttered, "but they're unlike any I've seen before. We certainly didn't include any of these in Gideon's book."

She would ask her husband about them. Mary gathered up the strange fossils and, her heart beating with excitement, headed back towards the patient's house. As she reached the gate, she saw her husband waiting.

Dr Mantell spotted his wife rushing towards him.

"Hello there, Mary. What's wrong? Has something happened?"

"I'm fine," she replied. "But I've found something I thought you'd be interested in. Look!" Mary showed her husband the strange fossils. "I found them by the road back there – they were in a pile of stones. I think they're fossils, but I've never seen any like them before."

"Well, hand them over and we'll soon see what they are," Doctor Mantell said confidently, taking the rocks into his hands for a closer look. His expression changed to puzzlement and then excitement as he examined them. "You're absolutely right, my dear. What a find! I've no idea what they are. Where did you come across them?"

Mary explained where she'd seen them and they immediately set off for the site. On the way, the doctor couldn't stop looking at the strange rocks, cupping them in his hands and holding them up to the light. What creature had they come from? He couldn't think of any that would solve the mystery.

Soon the couple found themselves near the piles of stones and the workmen.

"Excuse me," the doctor said. "Can I speak to your foreman?"

A large man appeared, wiping the sweat from his brow. "Aye sir, that's me. What can I do for you?"

"Well, I was wondering where these rocks came from? Did you dig them up from the road, or have you had them delivered?"

The foreman scratched his head. "Well sir, they come from hereabouts. We get them from the sandstone quarry nearby and we've had no complaints about them either."

"I'm sure you haven't. That's wonderful, thank you. Do you think you could direct us to this quarry?"

After noting the directions, the Mantells headed off towards the quarry. A plan was already forming in Dr Mantell's mind and he now shared it with his wife. "When we get to the quarry, I'll ask them to look out for any other unusual pieces of rock. If they do come across any more fossils then I'll take them to some experts I've read about. I have a feeling that we're on the verge of something big. You know, I think this could be the best day of our lives..."

The first part of Dr Mantell's plan worked, and another fossilized specimen was discovered in the quarry. But what happened next?

A. Dr Mantell showed the fossils to the experts of the day, claiming that they belonged to a giant species of animal that had become extinct. However, no one believed him, and as a result Dr Mantell gave up his interest in fossils and concentrated on medicine. His discovery only came to light years later, when the fossils were discovered among the rest of his collection.

B. The experts refused to believe the doctor's theory, but Mantell didn't give up. Eventually, having identified the fossils as resembling the teeth of a type of lizard called an iguana, he made his findings public. This didn't lead to fame and fortune, though. Mantell's wife left him and he was forced to sell off his fossil collection to avoid bankruptcy.

C. The experts were impressed by the fossils that Dr Mantell produced, and after a high profile conference, they identified them as the remains of a giant iguana. Dr Mantell was hailed at public meetings as a genius and he soon became extremely rich. He gave up medicine and devoted the rest of his life to studying fossils.

Answer: B

...espite the experts' disbelief, Dr Mantell continued to ...arch the newfound fossils. A chance encounter ...an expert on iguanas at the museum at the ...ollege of Surgeons led to him to realize that ...s resembled iguana teeth, although they ...larger than any previously found. This ...to Mantell's theory being accepted. In ...a public announcement describing his ...reptile of huge size. He called his ...opo... because of its link with the ...ell became more and more ...nd eventually died a lonely ...t spring day in 1822.

The
Altho
led
the
Ma
da

DID YOU KNOW?

Dr Gideon Mantell has gone down in history as the first person to discover the dinosaurs, but he didn't name them. That honour fell to the famous British scientist, Sir Richard Owen, when he made a speech on Friday 30th July 1841. By this time, so many fossilized remains had been unearthed that Owen proposed that an extinct group of reptiles had walked the earth millions of years before humankind. He called these animals dinosaurs, from the Greek *deinos* meaning "terrible" and *saurus* meaning "lizard".

first palaeontologists

Although it was Dr Mantell's interest in fossils that led him to discover Iguanodon's existence, he wasn't the first palaeontologist. Eleven years before Dr Mantell's discovery, Mary Anning, the 11-year-old daughter of a Lyme Regis shopkeeper, discovered the skeleton of an Ichthyosaurus, a large marine animal from the Jurassic period.

Mary Anning's spectacular find was just one of the things that made palaeontology increasingly popular. As more people took up fossil hunting, more fossils came to light and people began to ask questions such as: "How old are they?" and "Why don't they look like any other animals we know?"

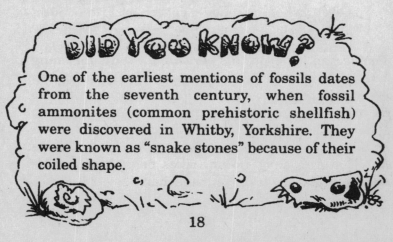

DID You KNOW?

One of the earliest mentions of fossils dates from the seventh century, when fossil ammonites (common prehistoric shellfish) were discovered in Whitby, Yorkshire. They were known as "snake stones" because of their coiled shape.

The first problems

Nowadays, if you've got a question about dinosaurs or life on earth you'll find shelves full of books about these subjects. But if you wanted any answers back in the early 1800s, there was only one book to read – the Bible. At this time, the Christian Church was the most powerful force in Europe, and most people believed exactly what the Bible said.

According to the Bible, God created heaven and earth and all the living things on it in six days – before having a well-deserved day off on Sunday. Unfortunately, human beings weren't very grateful for all God's hard work, and they began misbehaving. To punish them, God made a huge flood which washed everything away except for Noah, his family and the animals on the ark. When the flood waters receded, Noah landed his ark – and all the people and animals on earth today are descended from Noah's passengers.

People had believed this version of events for many hundreds of years (and some still do). But when geologists began to look at the earth and its fossils in more detail, they came up with their own theories. The Church wasn't exactly pleased when some people began to question its teaching. This is only natural, since no one likes being told they're wrong – just try it on your teacher!

As a result, battle lines were drawn up between the scientists and the Church.

IT'S SIMPLE – GOD CREATED THE EARTH. YOU'LL FIND THAT ITS SURFACE AND ALL THE NATURAL FORMATIONS ON IT WERE FORMED BY THE AFTERMATH OF A CATASTROPHIC FLOOD.

Charles Lyell (1797–1895) argued against these ideas in 1831:

MY OBSERVATIONS PROVE THAT NATURAL PROCESSES HAVE SHAPED THE EARTH OVER MILLIONS OF YEARS. THE WIND WEARS AWAY MOUNTAINS, VALLEYS ARE ERODED BY RIVERS, VOLCANOES ERUPT AND CREATE LARGER VOLCANOES, TIDES AND WAVES ERODE CLIFFS AND CHANGE THE SHORELINE. AS A RESULT I CONCLUDE THAT THERE WAS NO FLOOD AND THE EARTH IS MUCH OLDER THAN PREVIOUSLY THOUGHT.

As new theories about the creation of the earth took hold, palaeontologists also began to question the Church's explanation of where the fossilized remains of these unusual animals came from.

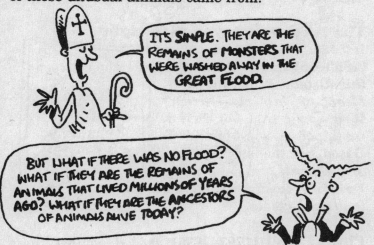

IT'S SIMPLE. THEY ARE THE REMAINS OF MONSTERS THAT WERE WASHED AWAY IN THE GREAT FLOOD.

BUT WHAT IF THERE WAS NO FLOOD? WHAT IF THEY ARE THE REMAINS OF ANIMALS THAT LIVED MILLIONS OF YEARS AGO? WHAT IF THEY ARE THE ANCESTORS OF ANIMALS ALIVE TODAY?

These questions were to spark some of the greatest scientific minds of the time into action. Scientists compared the fossilized bones with those of known animals and came up with ideas to explain the differences. After a few false starts, they came up with...

One theory that was close to the mark

Jean-Baptiste de Monet, Chevalier de Lamark (1744–1829), was a poor aristocrat with a rich interest in animals. He was convinced that the characteristics of animals and plants could develop to cope with changing surroundings and were then passed on to their offspring. Nowadays, many of Lamark's ideas are thought to be incorrect, but he was the first to suggest that animals could evolve and pass these changes on to the next generation. His theory, along with the books published by Charles Lyell, paved the way for...

The theory that was dead right

In 1859, Charles Darwin (1809–1882) published *On the Origin of Species by Means of Natural Selection*. It was a big title, but then it contained a very big idea. Based on his observations of animals and plants, Darwin's theory rested on four main points.

Point 1: Natural selection

Darwin realized that nature is a fairly nasty business – a case of eat or be eaten – and that only the cleverest or fastest animals or those best suited to their natural conditions have been able to survive.

Point 2: The same but different

Darwin noticed that the animals in all species were born with characteristics that gave them a better chance of survival. So, for example, animals with good camouflage had been able to survive predators better than those without it.

Point 3: Lots of babies

The animals best able to survive are more likely to leave the most offspring.

Point 4: Revolution

Each generation therefore includes increasingly better-adapted animals. Darwin's ideas explained why some animals changed their appearance over time, while those that hadn't evolved as succesfully died out.

Darwin's theory was so revolutionary (rather than evolutionary) that it took him not one, not two, but *twenty* years to publish it. It caused a huge uproar at the time, and some people still remain unconvinced today. However, his theory is important to the study of dinosaurs. When they were first discovered, most people accepted the Church's explanation that dinosaurs were giant monsters which lived before the flood. After the work of Darwin and other early scientists, though, palaeontologists began to study dinosaur remains scientifically. Nowadays they believe that dinosaurs evolved during the time they ruled the earth, and think that by studying modern animals, they can work out how dinosaurs once lived.

You might suppose that after early disagreements scientists would have become fed up with arguing with each other, but you'd be dead wrong. You'll soon discover that the arguments that started after Dr Mantell's discovery are still going strong, and that dinosaurs are continuing to drive palaeontologists potty.

DINOSAUR TIMES

Dinosaurs roamed the earth such a long time ago that one of the hardest things about them is imagining when they were alive. Try to think of something that happened ages ago (like the last time you got a pocket money rise). If that was two years ago, treble the time, multiply it by a thousand, double it, double it once more – and you'll still be way short of the mark.

In fact, the first dinosaurs evolved about 245 million years ago, and they survived for about 180 million years before suddenly dying out about 65 million years ago. Think of it this way – if the time that's passed since life began on earth were compressed into a one year diary, then life started on January 1st and the dinosaurs appeared on the 5th December before becoming extinct around 24th December. Humankind arrived late in the final minutes of December the 31st.

LIFE ON EARTH AS A YEAR.

BUDGE UP!

JAN FEB MAR APR MAY JUN JUL AUG SEP OCT NOV DEC

During the millions of years that the dinosaurs lived, the geography, the weather and the plants on earth changed, while many different kinds of dinosaur evolved, became extinct and were replaced by newer species. Palaeontologists can't give exact dates for when things happened, but the following pages give you an idea of what would have been hitting the headlines in dinosaur times!

· TRIASSIC TIMES ·

DATE: 245-280 MILLION YEARS AGO

A new age dawns

Welcome to the Triassic period and the dawn of what's certain to be a fascinating age. We predict big things for the dinosaurs – they're about to arrive and take over from earlier species.

Births and deaths

Early Triassic

Bad news as we say farewell to the therapsids. Sadly, these hairy, mammal-like reptiles have now died out. The good news is that we welcome to the Archosaurs, a group of small, lizard-like reptiles.

Profile: Lagosuchus

Name: Lagosuchus – a fairly typical early member of the Archosaur family.

Size: 30cms long

Favourite activity: hunting

Favourite food: insects and grubs

Features: Lagosuchus boasts sharp teeth, long legs and a slender body which is ideal for speedy hunting.

Mid-Triassic

It's time to say goodbye to the early Archosaurs, but welcome to a new kind of animal – the dinosaurs. Most of these early dinosaurs are predators.

Late Triassic

Welcome to the first kinds of herbivore, or plant-eating dinosaur, closely followed by...

Profile: Eoraptor

Name: Eoraptor – one of the earliest dinosaurs yet discovered.

Size: 1m long

Hobby: hunting

Favourite food: small reptiles

Features: Eoraptor claims to be an improved version of Lagosuchus. It is bigger and faster, with larger claws and teeth.

Profile:Anchisaurus

Name: Anchisaurus
– an early, plant-eating dinosaur.

Size: 2.5m long

Favourite food: plants

Features: Anchisaurus is particularly proud of its long neck. It also has strong arms with big curved thumb claws which are ideal for harvesting food from trees and bushes.

Triassic trtrends

The bigger the better seems to be the dinosaurs' motto. We've noticed a continuing increase in their size as they evolve, and this trend shows no sign of slowing down.

Weather report

The climate is generally warm and mild everywhere. Showers can be expected in coastal areas as winds pick up water from the seas, while inland areas will become hot and desert-like.

Travel corner

Roaming around remains easy for all dinosaurs as at this time earth has only one landmass (Editor's note: this supercontinent was later called Pangaea, meaning "all earth", by palaeontologists).

Travel tip – avoid the hot spots

Following the disappearance of numerous species, we advise that all dinosaurs should avoid travelling across the latest travel hot spots – the huge desert regions of Pangaea. Although no one knows exactly what happened to the missing animals (**Editor's note:** their bones were discovered in twisted positions by palaeontologists), drought and sudden sandstorms may well turn out to have killed them.

Nature news

We're delighted to introduce a new section to the paper. For all nature lovers, here's a picture showing a typical Triassic scene, with ferns growing beside lakes and streams, while monkey puzzle trees and other tall conifers thrive on drier land.

Competition corner

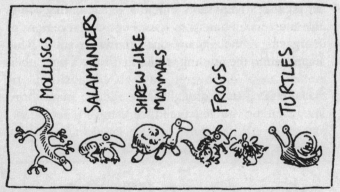

Why not enter our fun competition – can you match the names of some of the other animals around during the Triassic period to their pictures?

·JURASSIC TIMES·

DATE ~200–135 MILLION YEARS AGO

Dinosaurs rule the earth

Yes, it's official. Throughout the Jurassic period, dinosaurs have become the most dominant group of animals on earth. They've adapted to some of the changes in weather and geography better than any other group, and there are now more kinds of dinosaur than ever before. Can this success story continue? Watch this space.

Births and deaths

Early Jurassic

It's goodbye to the early small plant-eating dinosaurs, but let's say "hello" to the first large sauropods. We'd also like to welcome some new evolutionary arrivals, in the shape of Lesothosaurus and other small two-legged dinosaurs with bird-like feet.

Middle Jurassic

We've previously welcomed some large plant-eaters, and now it's the turn of the larger meat-eating members of the theropod family to appear.

Late Jurassic

Welcome to some even bigger plant-eaters. When Diplodocus becomes extinct, its place is taken by even larger animals. It's also time to greet the first stegosaurs.

Profile: Diplodocus

Name: Diplodocus – a member of the sauropod family
Size: 27m long
Favourite activity: eating
Favourite food: plants
Features: Diplodocus walks on all four legs. It has a long tail and a long neck which is perfect for reaching leaves on taller trees.

Profile: Allosaurus

Name: Allosaurus (means strange reptile), a powerful member of the theropod family

Size: 11m long

Favourite food: large plant-eating dinosaurs such as Stegosaurus

Features: Long tail, powerful feet and huge sharp claws.

Profile: Brachiosaurus

Name: Brachiosaurus, an enormous sauropod

Size: 23m long and 12m high

Favourite food: plants

Features: Sheer size and weight. Walking on four legs, Brachiosaurus tips the scales at over 40 tonnes (eight times heavier than a modern-day elephant).

Jurassic trends

There's no doubt that some dinosaurs are continuing to grow and grow. Brachiosaurus is big enough to put Diplodocus and any other previous dinosaur in the shade.

Weather report

The climate is generally warm and mild everywhere. However, more rain is forecast throughout, as the seas begin to erode coastal areas and spread inland over desert regions.

Travel corner

Travelling looks certain to become more difficult, as Pangaea breaks up into two continents. (Editor's note: scientists later called the northern landmass Laurasia, and the southern one, Gondwana.) To make getting about even trickier, erupting volcanoes will spew out great lava flows which cover parts of the land, while the sea will flood inland, creating new lakes and covering deserts. Instead of moving around, dinosaurs might be tempted to stay in their own areas and adapt to their new surroundings.

Travel tip –
beware sticky situations

If at all possible, tar pits should be avoided. Once caught, any struggles will only lead to a dinosaur sinking even deeper into the tar – guaranteeing a particularly sticky end.

Nature news

You might think that herbivores would get excited at the news that new plants such as horsetails are joining the ferns and trees on earth. However, when the latest plant arrivals were pointed out to them, the herbivores refused to make any comment – they were too busy eating them.

Competition corner

Are you an eagle-eyed animal spotter? Why not test your observation skills by seeing how many of the following animals (which lived side by side with the dinosaurs) you can spot.

Bees – these insect arrivals are beginning to make a buzz by the end of the Jurassic period.

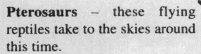

Shrew-like mammals – small and covered in hair, these creatures burrow into and climb over the planet's surface.

Plesiosaurs and ichthyosaurs – these sea creatures rule the waves.

Pterosaurs – these flying reptiles take to the skies around this time.

·CRETACEOUS TIMES·
DATE: 65 – 135 MILLION YEARS AGO

How long will the dinosaurs' reign continue? Forever seems to be the answer. It's now more than 100 million years since the very first dinosaurs appeared, and they just keep on coming. While certain types have become extinct, they have been replaced by newer, improved species. We've no doubt that the dinosaurs' success story is set to run and run.

Births and deaths

Early Cretaceous
It's goodbye to the enormous sauropods, and hello to many new kinds of dinosaur – including Ankylosaurus and Iguanodon, a member of the ornithopod family.

Iguanodon profile

Name: Iguanodon
Size: 9m high
Favourite activity: roaming around in huge herds of fellow Iguanodon
Favourite food: plants
Features: walks on two feet and uses its height to reach leaves in high trees. Has large thumb spikes.

Middle Cretaceous

New arrivals on the scene include the ceratopsian dinosaurs, but it's a hard time to be a herbivore as bigger, stronger and even better predators appear. These meat-eaters, such as Tyrannosaurus rex and Velociraptor, are members of the carnosaur and coelurosaur families.

Late Cretaceous

Hadrosaurs, pachycephalosaurs and members of the ceratopid family make their first appearances on earth.

Profile: Tyrannosaurus rex

Name: Tyrannosaurus rex
Size: 12m long
Favourite activity: hunting
Favourite food: Iguanodon and other plant-eating dinosaurs
Features: massive neck for ripping flesh from bones, huge finely serrated teeth for sawing through skin, and curiously small arms.

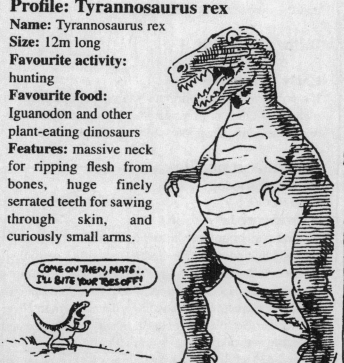

COME ON THEN, MATE.. I'LL BITE YOUR TOES OFF!

Profile: Pachycephalosaurus

Name: Pachycephalosaurus
Size: 8m long
Favourite food: plants
Features: incredibly thick skull decorated with knobs and spikes, possibly used to headbutt rivals.

Weather report

ONLY ANOTHER 100 MILLION YEARS UNTIL THEY INVENT THE UMBRELLA.

The climate continues to be very warm and mild, but wet and dry seasons arrive for the first time.

Travel corner

Travel plans continue to be disrupted as numerous changes take place. The landmasses continue to drift apart as Laurasia splits into three new continents – East Asia, North America and Euramerica. In addition, tropical jungles spring up and begin to cover the earth, while huge mountain ranges are formed and volcanic activity increases dramatically.

We would advise the cancellation of all non-urgent

trips, and suggest that each dinosaur species continues to adapt and evolve to suit its own location.

Travel tips – watch out for freaky floods and vicious volcanoes

Flash floods have been blamed for sweeping away large herds of plant-eaters in the continent of North America, and travelling dinosaurs should be alert to this danger unless they want their jumbled bones to be discovered millions of years from now.

Lava flows can normally be avoided by fast-moving dinosaurs, however erupting volcanoes offer an invisible threat from poisonous gases. Our advice – give volcanoes a wide berth.

Nature news

There's some bloomin' marvellous news just on for plant lovers everywhere, as the first flowering plants appear on earth.

Competition corner

These two pictures show an almost identical scene from the Cretaceous period, but we've removed some of the other animals that were around at the time. Can you spot the differences and find the missing animals? (Answers printed below)

1. Snakes slither into view during this period.
2. The largest-ever pterosaur, the massive Quetzalcoatlus, reaches for the sky.
3. Giant crocodile-like mosasaurs and long-necked plesiosaurs swim in the oceans.
4. Mammals are still small, shrew-like creatures which are mainly active at night.

STOP PRESS

DATE: 65 MILLION YEARS AGO.

Dinosaurs disappear!

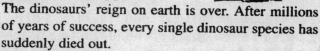

The dinosaurs' reign on earth is over. After millions of years of success, every single dinosaur species has suddenly died out.

Shocked survivors (including mammals, birds and turtles) cannot shed light on the mystery. "One minute they were there, the next few thousand years later, they'd all gone" is a typical comment.

Our journalists are investigating the reasons for this dreadful event, and we hope to bring you news in later editions.

FABULOUS FAMILIES

How would you describe a typical scientist (if you don't know any, just think about your science teacher)? Slightly bonkers, forgetful, totally scruffy? While most scientists tend to look fairly disorganized on the outside, one of the things they all share is a tidy mind.

As soon as they realized that dinosaurs weren't monsters and decided to study them scientifically, palaeontologists discovered that a monstrously difficult task lay ahead — grouping dinosaurs into families with shared characteristics. If you've ever tried to put your own family tree together, you'll know how hard that is — but imagine trying to build family trees for animals that died out millions and millions of years ago.

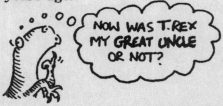

NOW WAS T.REX MY GREAT UNCLE OR NOT?

What's more, while it was fairly simple to place some dinosaurs with their cousins, other dinosaurs' relatives proved much harder to trace. Scelidosaurus is a large four-legged dinosaur that over the years has been adopted into the ankylosaur, stegosaur and ornithopod families by different scientists.

After lots of discussion, palaeontologists finally agreed that dinosaurs belonged to the following families. But there may well be a discovery just around the corner – or under the ground – that could throw everything by introducing an entirely new kind of dinosaur.

In the beginning

It all began with the **thecodontians** (see the Lagosuchus profile on page 25) in the early Triassic period. These animals were the forerunners of the dinosaurs, and from them, palaeontologists worked out that different dinosaur groups could be distinguished by their hip-bones.

One group, which had reptile-like hip-bones, were named **saurischians**. The other group, which were bird-hipped, were called the **ornithischians**. Easy isn't it? So far, so good.

The saurischians were divided into two groups – **theropods** and **sauropods**. Still keeping up? Great. Let's tackle the therapods first.

Theropods

You wouldn't want this lot to get their claws into you. Theropods were the first flesh-eating dinosaurs. They walked upright on two legs, hunted their prey, and had sharp teeth and claws for cutting through flesh. Weighing in at several tonnes and at 11m long, Allosaurus was a typical theropod.

The next generation

Over millions of years, the theropods evolved and divided into two improved versions, **carnosaurs** and **coelurosaurs**.

Carnosaurs (which means "flesh lizards") went for size and strength. They were still flesh-eaters who walked on two legs, but they were bigger and stronger than their theropod predecessors. Tyrannosaurus rex at 14m long and more than 6 tonnes, belonged to the carnosaur family.

By contrast, the **coelurosaurs** went down a different evolutionary route. Small and lightly built, they swapped size for speed and agility, but retained sharp teeth and cutting claws for flesh-eating. Compsognathus was no bigger than a cat, and counted Deinonychus and Velociraptor among its killer coelurosaur cousins.

Sauropods

Sauropods had the same reptile-like hip-bones as the theropods, but they were different in almost every other way. The sauropods (meaning "lizard feet") were herbivores, or plant-eaters. They walked on all four legs and seemed to believe that big is beautiful. Diplodocus, Supersaurus and Brachiosaurus were all enormous members of the sauropod family.

Bird-hipped dinosaurs

On the bird-hipped side, palaeontologists divide some of the most common dinosaurs into six different families. Ready? Here we go!

Ornithopods shared certain characteristics. They walked upright on two legs and were plant-eaters. Other dead give-aways to being an ornithopod were having a horned beak and bird-like feet. Iguanodon, the dinosaur discovered by Dr Gideon Mantell, was an ornithopod.

Hadrosaurs were also plant-eaters, but they were bigger than the ornithopods. Members of the hadrosaur family had duckbill-shaped mouths and huge crests on their heads.

Classifying **pachycephalosaurs** didn't cause palaeontologists too many headaches. These large, two-legged plant-eaters are known as bone-headed, not because they were stupid but because they had massively thick skulls.

Members of the **stegosaur** family also stick out like a sore thumb – they all had bony plates or spikes along their backs. Stegosaurs also had small heads and walked on four legs. Family members included Kentrosaurus.

Dinosaur spotters wouldn't have any trouble recognizing members of the **ankylosaur** family. The ankylosaurs were covered in hard, bony plates which gave them all the grace and elegance of a battle tank. They stomped around on four legs, while their look was completed by a spiky, armoured tail.

Ceratopians could be called the late developers of the dinosaur world, since they were the last kind to appear. They walked on four legs and had large horns and huge frills on their head. Despite their fierce appearance, these large dinosaurs were plant-eaters.

Dead difficult names

Having grouped the dinosaurs into families, scientists also had some tidying up to do when it came down to the names of individual dinosaurs.

Naming any animal or plant is a serious business and follows strict laws laid down by the globe-trotting Swedish zoologist, Carl Linnaeus (1707–78). As a result, each individual dinosaur is given a two-part scientific name, such as Tyrannosaurus rex.

The first name describes the genus (a Latin word meaning "race") and the second word describes the animals' species. To see how it works, let's compare Tyrannosaurus with a domestic cat.

Family: Felidae

Genus: *Felis*

Species: *domesticus*

Family: Carnosauria

Genus: *Tyrannosaurus*

Species: *rex*

47

The name given to an animal is normally chosen by the scientist who first describes the creature. This sounds simple enough, but in the rush to claim the credit for a discovery, many early palaeontologists named specimens without checking to see if anyone else had already found and named them.

DEAD AMAZING FACT

Pelorosaurus (meaning "monster lizard") was probably given more genus names than any other dinosaur. Between 1850 and 1900, the remains of this large sauropod were found at different sites scattered throughout England. Almost every discovery led to a new name – Chondrosteosaurus, Dinodocus, Eucamerotus, Gigantosaurus, Hoplosaurus, Ischyrosaurus and Morinosaurus were all dreamt up before the remains were closely examined, and scientists realized that the fossils were all of the same kind of dinosaur.

What's in a name?

Dinosaurs are given Latin names, not because it makes them long and difficult to spell, but because it's the standard language used by scientists.

When it comes to naming their finds, most palaeontologists aren't too daring and tend to stick to two guidelines:

1. Give the dinosaur a name that describes its appearance. So, Triceratops means "three-horned face".

2. Name the dinosaur after the place where it was found. Can you guess where the herbivorous Muttaburrasaurus was found? Yes, you're spot on – Muttaburra, in Australia.

However, in certain cases, these rules go out of the window. Can you match up each of the following dinosaurs with the reason why it received its unusual name.

A. Tianchisaurus nedegoapeferima
B. Diplodocus carnegii
C. Gasosaurus
D. Austrosaurus mckillopi

1. Named after the owner of the land where the dinosaur was found.
2. Named after a particular industry's contribution to palaeontology.
3. Named after the person who funded the dig.
4. Named to honour a famous film director.

Answers: A4, B3, C2, D1

A4. After Steven Spielberg (the director of the movie *Jurassic Park*) donated millions of dollars to Chinese palaeontologists, the species name of this member of the ankylosaur family was created from the first two letters of the surnames of the film's stars.

B3. Andrew Carnegie was a multimillionaire dinosaur hunter who paid for many dinosaur digs. His wife's name proved to be similarly inspirational to the palaeontologists who discovered Apatosaurus louisae.

C2. Gasosaurus was a 4m-long meat-eater that was found in China and named in 1985, after the gas industry had pumped large amounts of money into palaeontology.

D1. Mr McKillop was an Australian ranch owner who gave permission for a dig to take place on his land. Maiasaura peeblesorum was given its name for the same reason.

FANTASTIC FOSSILS

You don't have to be brain of Britain to realize that there's one big problem for anyone interested in dinosaurs. How do you find out about animals that have been dead for millions of years?

The answer, of course, lies with fossils. To the untrained eye, fossils may look just like lumps of old rock – but they are truly fantastic. Without them, no one would ever have known that the dinosaurs even existed.

Fantastic fossil fact file

1. The word fossil comes from the Latin fossilis and literally means "dug up".

2. Dinosaur fossils are nothing new – they've been around for hundreds of years. But until palaeontologists realized where fossils had come from, nobody really knew what they had found.

3. Ancient Chinese medicine books mention "dragon's teeth" and "dragon's eggs", which were almost certainly dinosaur fossils, while the Aboriginal legend of the emu-man is based on three-toed footprints found in rocks in Australia. In Europe, large bones were believed

to be the remains of unicorns, while a gigantic Megalosaurus thigh-bone led to some pretty tall tales when it was discovered in England in 1677. The bone was shown to Robert Plot who, despite being an Oxford professor, first said that it came from an elephant, before concluding that it had belonged to a gigantic human being.

Fantastic fossil forming

Of course, we now know that fossils come from animals that once roamed the earth, and we also know a lot more about how fossils were made. In most cases, making a fossil isn't fantastically difficult – it just takes a fantastically long time.

Step 1. Take one dead dinosaur and place corpse on sand or mud.

Step 2. Allow scavengers, wind and rain to help the skin decay, until you're just left with the dinosaur's skeleton.

Step 3. Let the mud or sand cover the exposed bones. Add more and more layers on top, then drip water over and allow it to seep through the layers.

Allow plenty of time for this stage. Approximately 70 million years will be ideal. Over this time, the minerals in the water will seep into the tiny spaces in the bones and fossilize them. Don't worry if the minerals dissolve the bones. If this happens, you will still be left with bone-shaped hollows or moulds that can be filled with plaster of Paris to reveal the exact shape of the missing bones.

WARNING
DO NOT UNCOVER THE BONES BEFORE THEY FOSSILIZE AS THEY MAY BE WASHED AWAY OR TURN TO DUST.

Step 4. Once the bones have been fossilized, gradually introduce rain and wind over the next few million years. This will erode the covering layers of mud, sand and rock, revealing the fossilized remains below.

The bare bones

Bones are one of the hardest parts of the body, which is why dinosaur bones (along with teeth and claws) are some of the most common fossils around. While you might think that a single bone couldn't tell you much about how dinosaurs lived, they've revealed some dead amazing facts.

DEAD AMAZING FACT 1

Dinosaurs weren't always as healthy as some Hollywood film makers think. From a study of fossilized bones, scientists have discovered that dinosaurs suffered from illnesses like arthritis, tumours and bacterial infections. These things probably didn't directly kill the dinosaurs, but any dinosaur that was slowed up by an illness was probably finished off by predatory dinosaurs.

DEAD AMAZING FACT 2

Palaeontologists were surprised to discover that many dinosaurs had broken bones during their lives, but eventually concluded that the fractures weren't caused by clumsiness but by arguments. Just like modern-day animals, dinosaurs probably fought among themselves, as well as with other species.

DEAD AMAZING FACT 3

By comparing the growth rings in the bones of dinosaurs, scientists have worked out that individual dinosaurs could have lived to be 100 years old – even older than your parents. Using this method, scientists estimated that some of the biggest sauropods might even have lived for a mind-boggling 200 years – even longer than your head teacher!

Terrific traces

Palaeontologists aren't just interested in fossilized bones – any trace of a dinosaur is terrific. Palaeontologists go potty if they find dinosaur footprints, eggs or even dung – they've even dreamt up new names for each of these things. Can you match the palaeontologists' name to the terrific trace?

A. Dinosaur eggs
B. Dinosaur dung
C. Fossilized footprints

1. Ichnites
2. Ooliths
3. Coprolites

Answers: A2, B3, C1

A. There was one big problem about the discovery of the first ooliths – how to get a look inside them. In the early days, X-ray machines were used, but now palaeontologists pop ooliths into a CAT scanner (short for computerized axial tomography). These machines give a clear picture of what's inside the egg and have revealed the fossilized remains of baby dinosaurs.

With the help of CAT scanners, scientists have found out a great deal about dinosaur babies from ooliths. In lots of ways they were similar to human babies – noisy, messy and smelly – but there were some important differences.

DID YOU KNOW?

1. Newborn dinosaurs were even funnier-looking than human babies. Relative to their full-grown size, their heads and eyes were big, while their limbs, necks and tails were short.

2. Baby dinosaurs knew that if they stayed small, they were in big trouble – so many of them grew up to be very big indeed. Mussaurus was about 28cm

long when it was born, but was over 150 times that size by the time it was fully grown. If your little brother or sister grew at the same rate, they'd reach a height of around 60m.

B. You might think that dinosaur dung sounds like a really revolting relic, but palaeontologists can't wait to get their hands on coprolites. A close examination of these rotten relics can indicate the size of a dinosaur's intestines, and also reveal its favourite food.

Before they get their hands really dirty, palaeontologists introduce the petrified poo to a bath of hydrochloric acid. The acid eats through the rocks and minerals surrounding the poo before stopping at the tough outer coating of plants.

A quick look through the microscope at the mulchy mush left behind lets palaeontologists get a sneak preview of what the dinosaur had for its last meal. The results have sometimes been surprising and have proved that most dinosaurs were anything but fussy eaters.

C. Fossilized footprints can reveal lots of fabulous dinosaur facts, and a discovery is immediately followed by a step-by-step investigation.

STEP 1. HOW MANY FEET? THE NUMBER OF FOOTPRINTS MADE BY AN INDIVIDUAL DINOSAUR TELLS PALAENTOLOGISTS WHETHER THE DINOSAUR WALKED ON TWO LEGS OR FOUR.

LOOK! FOOTPRINTS.... I'D SAY IT WAS A TWO-LEGGED CREATURE.

STEP 2. COUNT THE PRINTS. A LARGE NUMBER OF PRINTS MADE BY SIMILAR KINDS OF DINOSAUR INDICATES A HERD TRAVELLING TOGETHER

IT WAS TRAVELLING WITH A COMPANION.

STEP 3. MEASURE THE DISTANCE BETWEEN PRINTS TO WORK OUT HOW FAST THE DINOSAUR MAY HAVE BEEN MOVING.

AT ABOUT WALKING PACE.

STEP 4. IDENTIFICATION. EXAMINE THE FOOTPRINTS TO SEE IF THEY MATCH ANY KNOWN CLAWS OR FEET.

CAN YOU TELL WHAT IT IS?

YES. A THICK-HEADED DINOSAUR HUNTER!

DID YOU KNOW?

By examining fossilized footprints, palaeontologists have worked out that some dinosaurs could move amazingly fast. As well as being one of the meanest dinosaurs that ever lived, Allosaurus was also one of the speediest. It's estimated that this predator could run at about 40km/h. This means that in a race the dinosaur would have beaten the world's fastest human by a head – and an arm and a leg.

Scaly skin

One of the rarest traces of a dinosaur is a piece of fossilized flesh or an impression of scaly skin. This is made when the skin of the dead dinosaur rots away, but its imprint on the ground fossilizes. Unfortunately, although these imprints reveal that dinosaur skin was tough and scaly, no one can say for sure what colour dinosaurs were or what markings they had. The best conclusion scientists have reached is that the most successful survival tactic would have been for dinosaurs to be a similar colour to their surroundings, so that they were camouflaged.

Amazing Archaeopteryx

These imprints have certainly made some big impressions on palaeontologists, and none have been bigger than the one unearthed with Archaeopteryx. The discovery of this dinosaur has caused one of the biggest palaeontological arguments ever.

When was Archaeopteryx found? The first skeleton was discovered in a quarry in Germany in 1861.

And what was so amazing about it? Well, the discovery showed a perfectly preserved, extraordinary fossilized imprint. Instead of scaly skin, Archaeopteryx was covered in feathers!

Why did people get in flap about that? Until then, no one thought that dinosaurs had feathers.

I suppose you're going to say that palaeontologists were tickled pink by the discovery. Very good, but unfortunately that's not the case.

Why not? When Archaeopteryx was studied carefully, it revealed some remarkable facts.

Such as? Although it was covered in feathers like a bird, Archaeopteryx had a very similar bone structure to small dinosaurs like Compsognathus, as well as other reptilian features such as a long bony tail and clawed fingers.

Which means? Scientists concluded that this dinosaur was part-bird and part-reptile.

And is that so remarkable? It certainly is. As it had the skeleton of a dinosaur but the feathers of a bird, scientists suggested that Archaeopteryx was the missing link in the evolutionary chain connecting dinosaurs and present-day birds.

How did this happen? Well, the theory is that early birds and small meat-eating dinosaurs like Compsognathus had almost identical skeletons. Over millions of years, feathers evolved from scales, then the dinosaur lost its teeth and clawed fingers. Its solid bones became hollow and its arms became wings, until eventually it was ready to fly.

I see. And what's so important about that? Well, if birds were descended from dinosaurs, it's quite likely that they shared similar characteristics.

Can you give me an example? Here's two for starters. Birds are warm-blooded and able to move quickly – dinosaurs may well have been the same.

OK, I've got it now. So the discovery of Archaeopteryx was definite proof that dinosaurs are closely related to birds. That must have made everyone happy. Unfortunately not. Other scientists have had very different views on Archaeopteryx.

Go ahead then. One scientist simply explained it as a freak bird.

I assume that some clever clogs shot this idea down. You're spot on. A sharp-eyed palaeontologist took a chunk out of this theory by pointing out that Archaeopteryx had a full set of teeth in its beak – which is a feature of reptiles rather than birds.

But that didn't stop others from trying? Right again. Andreas Wagner claimed that the animal was a reptile that had somehow independently acquired feathers.

That sounds a bit far-fetched. It's not as far-fetched as his next move. He tried to rename the dinosaur Griphosaurus, claiming that it was a griffin – a legendary monster with the head and wings of an eagle, and the body of a lion.

Enough said. Has anyone else had a go at Archaeopteryx? They certainly have. Sir Fred Hoyle suggested that Archaeopteryx was a fake.

What? You mean that it was a counterfeit fossil? Exactly. He claimed that scientists had made a fake fossil to prove their theories of evolution.

FAKE! I'VE NEVER BEEN SO INSULTED. FRAUD!

I bet that made him popular. You lose, I'm afraid. The professor's ideas have often got him into hot water. On one occasion, he even had to have Special Branch protection to give a lecture at The Royal Institution in London.

And what happened to his suggestion? Extensive tests have shown the fossil to be genuine.

But couldn't the tests be flawed? There's also the little problem that five more complete skeletons of Archaeopteryx have been found.

And that's it? For now. No other suggestions have really taken off, but you never know what might happen in the future.

DID YOU KNOW?

The row about whether birds are the direct descendants of dinosaurs looks set to run and run. Some scientists think that Archaeopteryx is a fake, while others think that its discovery fits the evolutionary theory just too conveniently. Yet others believe that Archaeoperyx can't be a descendant of the dinosaurs, for the simple reason that the dinosaurs haven't died out.

So far, no species of dinosaur has been found alive, but it hasn't stopped people from looking. In fact, the search for dinosaurs and other mythical creatures has even been given the scientific name Cryptozoology. Cryptozoologists claim that the dragons mentioned in British, Norse and Asian myths are evidence that some dinosaurs survived the mass extinction at the end of the Cretaceous period. Currently, the most popular creatures being studied by cryptozoologists are sea serpents and large aquatic creatures that have allegedly been sighted in lakes. Some people claim these creatures are plesiosaurs which have survived from dinosaur times by living in deep cold water.

We've all heard of the Loch Ness Monster, but "Nessie" may have cousins all over the world, including several lakes in America, Russia and even Africa. In 1990, a British explorer called Redmond O'Hanlon led an expedition through the jungle to try to find the lake-dwelling Congo dinosaur. The expedition was not a great success – the explorers saw lots of deep dark jungle, but there was no sign of a dinosaur and the only thing O'Hanlon caught was a disease called malaria.

FOOD, GLORIOUS FOOD

Dinosaur diets

Ask your best friend to open his or her mouth and what do you see? Some teeth that are sharp and pointy for stripping flesh, and some that are flat on top for eating your greens. Humans are omnivores (which means that we can eat both meat and plants) and our teeth have evolved accordingly. However, the dinosaurs were divided into two different types – carnivores (which only ate flesh) and herbivores (whose diet consisted of plants) – and their teeth were perfectly adapted to their diet.

Luckily, teeth were one of the hardest parts of the dinosaurs' bodies and fossilized teeth are regularly uncovered. As a result, studying dinosaurs' teeth has become a very juicy subject, which has opened the world of dinosaur diets wide open.

WELL I NEVER!

Dental deductions

A dinosaur's teeth are a dead give-away when it comes to deciding whether the owner was a harmless herbivore or a killer carnivore. Why not take part in our dinosaur tooth quiz and see how sharp you are? Put yourself in a dinosaur's shoes and remember that dental deductions were a matter of life and death.

A large dinosaur appears close by. It opens its jaws to reveal a mouth filled with hundreds of teeth. Will you stay and count them, or run for the hills?

Answer: You'll be quite safe if you stay put. Some herbivores had hundreds of teeth which they used for grinding up plants. Edmontosaurus's toothy smile was made up of over 1,000 teeth.

A few minutes later, you come across a tooth that's curved like a dagger. It's just fallen from the mouth of a nearby dinosaur. Is it safe to stay put or should you beat a rapid retreat?

Answer: If you don't get the point of these curved teeth then you'll be in serious trouble. Carnivores like Allosaurus had more than 60 curved teeth which were specially designed for ripping into flesh.

Another huge dinosaur appears. A short row of sharp, pencil-shaped teeth are visible in the front of its mouth. Are you facing a herbivore or carnivore?

Answer: A herbivore – Diplodocus used the row of teeth at the front of its mouth to strip vegetation from trees.

From among the trees, a different dinosaur appears. You can see that its teeth are shaped like spoons. Are you going to be next on the menu or is it safe to stay put?

Answer: You'll be quite safe where you are. Amygdalodon's spoon-shaped teeth were perfect for spooning vegetation into its body.

A small dinosaur arrives on the scene. You can just make out two rows of serrated teeth in its mouth. Do you ignore the newcomer or run for it?

Answer: You'd better get going. Serrated teeth were a dead give-away. Only carnivores had these teeth that were perfect for cutting through flesh.

Dead interesting dental fact

Dinosaurs always had new teeth growing below the ones in use, and T-rex could grow an entire new set of 50 teeth within just two or three years!

Extraordinary equipment

Teeth weren't the only difference between carnivores and herbivores. As different plant- and meat-eaters evolved, they became even better equipped to forage for their particular food.

DID YOU KNOW?

Mamenchisaurus was a herbivore with a huge neck. At 22m long (its neck was 10m long), this dinosaur is thought to have stood in the middle of a pond or lake and used its neck like a giant vacuum cleaner to hoover up the plants on all sides.

The claws of some carnivores were particularly well adapted for going in for the kill. Baryonyx is the only carnivore that's known to have been hooked on fish – scientists think that it used its huge curved claw to spear its favourite food.

Velociraptors had an ingenious switchback claw on their second toe. When running, the claw was flicked harmlessly out of the way, but it could be switched into slashing position for an attack.

Some scientists think that other carnivores may also have had a secret weapon. It's thought that even a quick nip would be fatal, as the bacteria from rotting meat in their mouths would quickly poison their victims.

Grisly guzzling

Awesome appetites

Scientists estimate that big carnivores like Tyrannosaurus rex needed to eat an enormous 135kg of meat a day to survive. Yet even these massive meals would have looked like snacks compared to the intake of huge sauropods like Brachiosaurus and Supersaurus. These dinosaurs loved their greens so much that they'd tuck into a mind-boggling tonne of food each day.

ANY CHANCE OF SOME SALAD CREAM?

Huge helpings
Allosaurus' mouth was big to begin with, but it had a clever way of eating even huger helpings of its victims. Its jaws were loosely hinged so that it could bolt down massive mouthfuls of meat after each bite.

Crème cannibal
A fossilized Coelophysis was found to contain the bones of one its own young – a grisly guzzler indeed.

Not so fussy eater
When the stomach of one hadrosaur was examined, it was found to contain the remains of its last meal – a particularly indigestible concoction of bark, branches, pine cones and conifer needles.

Stone me
Despite their awesome appetites, sauropods had very few teeth. To make up for their lack of molars, and to help them digest tough plants, they swallowed round pebbles which they stored in their gut. These "gastroliths" then worked like mini-millstones to grind up food into a thick mulch so it could be digested. One Barosaurus was so keen on getting these stones down its neck that it had swallowed 64 of them.

Noxious noshing
The result of so much herbivorous nosh would have been obvious to anyone downwind of a plant-eater. Digesting such huge amounts of plants would have also produced huge amounts of natural gas.

Survival strategies

While a dinosaur's teeth and bones can prove conclusively if it was a carnivore or a herbivore, it's much harder to work out how the dinosaur behaved when it was alive. Other fossilized evidence such as footprints can offer some clues, but palaeontologists also study wild animals to help them make educated guesses about how the dinosaurs lived and died.

DEAD AMAZING FACT

Finding evidence of dinosaurs in action is very rare, but in 1971 an awesome discovery was made in Mongolia. Palaeontologists unearthed a Velociraptor and a Protoceratops locked together in a duel to the death. The carnivore was holding the bony head-frill of Protoceratops and slashing at its belly with its claw, while the herbivore had pierced Velociraptor's chest with its spiked head. They'd killed each other at exactly the same moment – which had been frozen in time for millions of years.

Herbivores and carnivores had very different survival strategies. For herbivores, finding enough plants to eat probably wasn't a major problem. Their main aim was to avoid ending up as the main course for any passing carnivore. But how *did* they survive attacks from marauding meat-eaters?

The herbivore's guide to survival

Happy herding
Dinosaurs knew that there was safety in numbers, and Iguanodon would gather in huge herds. While the young and their mothers stayed safely in the middle, large males patrolled the edges of the herd, their sharp thumb claws at the ready. Any Iguanodon that couldn't keep up with the moving herd would be left behind – in big danger from lurking carnivores.

Vicious circle

If threatened, the largest members of ceratopsian herds formed a defensive circle with their horns pointing outwards at the enemy, while the rest of the herd sheltered behind them.

Maiasaura mothers

These 9m-long herbivores laid their eggs in huge nests which they covered in rotting vegetation. This may sound like a rotten thing to do, but the heat produced by the decomposing plants kept the eggs warm while the dinosaurs inside grew. Instead of being tied to sitting on their nests, Maiasaura mothers were free to guard them. Once the eggs hatched, mothers only left their babies to fetch food for them. But even then, other mothers guarding nearby nests would have been around to defend the babies.

Quick getaway

Individual herbivores didn't put themselves on a plate for any passing predator. The strong legs of Hypsilophodon and the ostrich-like dinosaurs such as Ornithomimus made them champion sprinters and hurdlers. If it looked like they were for the high jump, they'd try to kick their way out of trouble.

Marine manouevres

From trails of fossilized footprints, palaeontologists have deduced that large sauropods would occasionally escape predators by taking to the water.

Frightening flares

If you've ever been unlucky enough to see photos of people flapping around in horrible 1970s' flared trousers, you can imagine the terrifying effect that Ouranosaurus made when it flared the large sail on its back. This shock tactic would have been enough to frighten most predators away.

Hard hides

It didn't take long for dinosaurs to realize that looking like a megaburger and chips on legs wasn't a good idea. Instead, they decided to make themselves as tough and unappetizing as school dinners. Stegosaurus decided to be a right pain to any carnivore and grew tough, spiky spines on its back, shoulders and tail. Meanwhile the bony studs that stuck out of the backs of Scelidosaurus would have given predators something to chew on.

Deadly defences

Even if the worse came to the worst and they were trapped by a predator, not all herbivores were dead meat. The fiercest carnivores would soon discover that their dinner wasn't going to give itself up without a fight.

DID YOU KNOW?

Diplodocus was quite capable of lashing out at attackers with its 3·5m-long tail, while the sharp spiky tails of Kentrosaurus and Stegosaurus would have been a real pain in any predator's neck.

The herbivore Euoplocephalus had a huge bony club at the end of its tail which weighed around 30kg. When swung around, it formed a extremely effective piece of self-defence. A single blow on target would have been enough to knock even the largest T-rex off balance, and it would certainly have put a predator off its intended victim for a long while.

Triceratops believed that attack was the best form of defence. If it was in trouble, it could put its horns down and charge – just like a modern-day rhinoceros. With a fully-grown Triceratops weighing in at around 5 tonnes, this really was the charge of the heavy brigade.

Happy hunting

For carnivores, there was no such thing as convenience food. If a meat-eater wanted to grab a bite to eat, that's exactly what it had to do – dinner would be running around and the survival of even the deadliest dinosaur depended on its ability to catch its next victim.

Here are some secrets of their happy hunting techniques.

Pack attack

One fossilized find of the 1960s was the bones of a huge herbivore, Tenontosaurus, near to the remains of four smaller Deinonychus – part of the pack of predators that had killed it.

Temporary teamwork

Predators weren't afraid to team up with other carnivores, and fossilized footprints have shown that even top hunters like Allosaurus and Velociraptors attacked in packs. They probably charged herds of sauropods, scattering the older males and looking for weak or young animals to kill. However, once their prey had been brought down, it was likely that the teamwork was at an end – it would then be each predator for itself.

Patient predators

A fantastic find in the American state of Texas confirmed that some dinosaurs were patient predators. The find consisted of two sets of footprints. One set was from a large Brontosaurus, while the other belonged to a smaller three-toed dinosaur, probably a predatory Allosaurus.

The tracks followed each other, and palaeontologists think that they are direct evidence of a carnivore stalking its prey. The patient predator would almost certainly have been rewarded at the end of its stalking, as it could have choosen the perfect time to move in for the kill.

Scavenger surprise

Most evidence has suggested that carnivores hunted down their prey, but scientists were in for a surprise when they excavated dried-up tar pits in Utah. Here they uncovered hundreds of bones from herbivores such as Diplodocus, along with the remains of carnivores like Allosaurus.

The find may show that carnivores weren't always predators, but would turn to scavenging if given half a chance. Attracted by the cries of trapped herbivores, the meat-eaters may have found themselves stuck in the tar when they attacked their prey.

T-rex on trial

The scavenging evidence surprised some scientists so much that they began to wonder if the carnivores really were predators. Could they actually have been scavengers who didn't hunt down their prey but just polished off animals that were already dead or wounded? To test their theory, the scientists set

their sights on the largest target they could find –
Tyrannosaurus rex...

More terrifying than a French test, scarier than
bungee jumping or a room full of great aunts,
Tyrannosaurus rex had been the undisputed
carnivore champion of the prehistoric world since it
was first discovered in 1902.

T-rex is the most massive meat-eater found so far.
Over 6m high, with 18cm-long razor-sharp teeth, it
certainly lived up to its name – Tyrannosaurus rex
means "tyrant lizard king". Its reputation as the
deadliest dinosaur had gone unchallenged until
palaeontologists took a good look at its remains and
decided to put its predatory skills to the test.

Other scientists immediately sprang to the
dinosaur's defence, and the trial began. Before you
look at both sides of the argument and decide
whether you think T-rex was a predator or a
scavenger, let's go back a few hundred million years
ago to a reconstruction of a typical attack...

TIME: DAWN. MID CRETACEOUS PERIOD.

SUDDENLY, T. REX LAUNCHES A LIGHTENING-FAST ATTACK!

T. REX STRIKES

IT'S ALL OVER IN ONE BITE.

GNASH!

CENSORED
GUZZLING TOO GRUESOME

But was it really like that? The dinosaur's defence team certainly think so, but the prosecuting palaeontologists have their own evidence.

Defence palaeontologist 1:

"T-rex was the perfect predator. My evidence shows that its powerful legs were capable of speeds of up to 40km/h. This turn of speed could only be sustained for short sprints, but it would have been enough to ambush prey."

Prosecution palaeontologist 1:

"Our studies show that T-rex's shin and thigh bones are about the same length, like those of humans. This suggests that it couldn't run any faster than 24km/h and that it could easily have been outpaced by its prey. In addition, we have calculated that T-rex's high centre of gravity meant that it lost its balance easily. If it turned a corner too quickly, it would topple over and have serious

trouble getting up again. T-rex wasn't agile enough to be a predator."

Defence palaeontologist 2:

"That's rubbish. We've compared its bite with that of a modern predator – a lion – and our tests have shown that T-rex's bite was over three times as powerful. Such biting power would only have been useful if a predator needed to dispatch a live victim quickly"

Prosecution palaeontologist 2:

"We've done our own comparison. The part of T-rex's brain that relates to smell is bigger than any creature on earth, except the turkey vulture – a well-known scavenger. What's more, although T-Rex's arms could lift a load of up to 185kg, they could only rotate 5cm at the elbow. This proves that they weren't designed for grasping live prey, but for scavenging flesh from dead dinosaurs."

The verdict?

The scientific jury is still out in the trial of Tyrannosaurus rex, but you can try to decide for yourself. Was T-rex a premier league predator, or do you think it should be renamed Scavengersaurus rex?

The argument looks set to run and run, but who knows, a new discovery or a new theory may come to light, thanks to the work of people who are mad about dinosaurs – the potty palaeontologists...

POTTY PALAENTOLOGISTS

Bone hunters, dinosaur detectives, palaeontologists, whatever you want to call them, they all have one quality in common – they're completely potty about dinosaurs.

To find out just how potty you would have to be to take on their job, simply answer the following question. Given the choice, which of the following alternatives would you prefer?

A. To win first prize in the lottery.
B. To spend a few minutes in the company of a live T-rex.

If you answered A, you're far too sensible to be a palaeontologist. If you answered B, you're completely potty – congratulations, you've got exactly what it takes!

Potty palaeontologist hall of fame
This complete pottiness was obvious in even the earliest palaeontologists.

William Buckland (1764–1856)
William Buckland was the first professor of geology at Oxford University. He has gone down in history for identifying a jumble of fossilized remains as belonging to a large, meat-eating dinosaur

which he named Megalosaurus (giant reptile).

Megalosaurus has since become known as the "waste basket" kind of dinosaur, as for many years any large meat-eaters' bones were classified as belonging to it. Buckland was also a kind of human dustbin – he was a great practical joker who was famous for eating absolutely anything, including slug soup and rhinoceros pie. He also turned up at parties with an unusual guest – his pet bear.

Sir Richard Owen (1804–92)

Richard Owen was the first person to give dinosaurs their name (see page 17). To celebrate the discovery of the dinosaurs and to show everyone just how potty he was, in 1852 Owen was put in charge of recreating life-sized versions of dinosaurs in the grounds of London's Crystal Palace (where they can still be seen).

It took a year to finish the reconstructions, and to mark the event, Owen invited 19 dignitaries to a feast – held inside the stomach of an Iguanodon. To ensure the event got off to a flying start, Owen even sent out invitations printed on a card in the shape of a pterodactyl's wing.

Ferdinand Hayden (1829–87)

In 1856, American geologist Ferdinand Hayden's pottiness actually saved his life. He was delighted to have discovered the first known dinosaur bones in North America, but was less happy to find that they were in Sioux Indian territory.

When Hayden was captured by warriors on the warpath, they were amazed to find out that he wasn't carrying a gun, just lumps of old rock. The Indian chief decided that if Hayden thought the rocks were valuable he was obviously crazy, and set him free with the words:

GO ON YOUR WAY, MAN WHO PICKS UP STONES WHILE RUNNING.

Roy Chapman Andrews (1884–1960)

Roy Chapman Andrews took up palaeontology after studying whales during World War I – while being a

spy for the Allies on the side. During his expeditions to the Mongolian Desert, he fought off snakes and bandits while surviving temperatures of 60°C, yet still had time to find the first dinosaur eggs, as well as remains of Velociraptor and Saurornithoides.

Although Andrews had his faults – he was so ham-fisted at digging out fossils that researchers back at his museum refer to any damaged specimen as having been "RCA-ed" – he was so inspirational that he became the model for the world-famous film character, Dr Indiana Jones.

Roland Bird

Modern-day palaeontologist Roland Bird wouldn't even let a small thing like death get in the way of his pottiness. So that everyone knew just how dead keen on dinosaurs he was, he insisted that his tombstone should be carved in the shape of a Brontosaurus.

Beyond the pale-aeontologists

Among all the potty palaeontologists, there were two who were slightly pottier than everyone else. This dinosaur-mad duo lived in the United States and went hunting for bones in some of the wildest parts of the Wild West. The rivalry between the two was so rotten that their antics were soon known as the "bone wars". These palaeontologists who went beyond the pale were called Edward Cope (1840–97) and Othniel Marsh (1831–99).

MARSH

COPE

A really rotten rivalry – ten terrific facts

1. Edward Cope was born in Philadelphia. He was a Quaker who became a professor at the University of Pennsylvania. At the age of six he saw a fossilized 30m-long sea creature called Hydrarchus. Although the fossil turned out to be a fake, it triggered Cope's ambition to become the world's greatest palaeontologist...

2. ...which was an ambition shared by Othniel Charles Marsh. Marsh came from a rich family. He fixed his own appointment as the first professor of palaeontology at Yale in 1860 by persuading a wealthy uncle to give the university a Natural History museum – with him as the director.

3. The pair's rotten rivalry began in 1868 when Cope published a description of the marine reptile, Elasmosaurus. The description contained some awful mistakes – Cope had even put the head at the wrong end – which Marsh immediately noticed and pointed out to Cope.

4. Cope accepted that he'd made mistakes and decided to buy up all the copies of the description. He bought all the copies that had been published – except for the two that Marsh possessed. Marsh refused to sell them.

5. Cope never forgave Marsh, and the potty palaeontologists began searching throughout the western United States, each trying to find more dinosaurs than the other. Between them, the dotty duo identified over 130 dinosaur species and found remains of Allosaurus, Apatosaurus, Diplodocus, Stegosaurus and Hadrosaurus, among others.

6. Cope and Marsh were in such a rush to take the credit for their latest dinosaur find that they rarely checked whether their rival had already found a similar one. Often, they would both publish details of the same dinosaur but with a different name.

7. They didn't let small things like wars between pioneers and Native Americans stand in their way. On one occasion, Cope was surrounded by braves on the warpath, but saved the day by taking out his false teeth several times. The braves looked on in amazement and didn't attack – they obviously didn't want to bite off more than they could chew.

8. Marsh tried to avoid similar teething troubles with Native Americans by negotiating his own truces. After one particularly successful bout of peace talks, a Sioux Indian chief called Red Cloud gave him an escort of his own warriors.

9. The mere thought of his rival had an explosive effect on Cope. After excavating a site, he would dynamite it to prevent Marsh from working the area.

10. The rotten rivalry lasted until Edward Cope died. Even then Cope managed to have the last word in insults – he had named one mammal fossil *Anisconchus cophater*, which translates as "the jagged-toothed Cope-hater".

Dead useful rocks

Although Cope and Marsh weren't very good at getting on with each other, they were very good at discovering dinosaurs. Unfortunately, this isn't always an easy thing to do. Old fossils usually don't just sit around waiting to be unearthed – except in your school staffroom.

Eagle-eyed palaeontologists can recognize the sort of rocks that contain fossils and, with the help of our Dead useful rock guide, so can you.

Dead Useful Rock Guide

Rocks are classified as coming in three categories – Metamorphic, Igneous and Sedimentary. Unfortunately, the sort of rock cakes you get at Great Aunt Ida's house don't count, even though they can have similar effects.

So how are they made?

Igneous rocks such as granite are cooked at high temperatures in volcanoes before being blasted out as lava. They never contain fossils. Sometimes, volcanic ash or cooling lava can trap animals which eventually get fossilised.

Sedimentary rocks are created when deposits of sand or mud build up and are gradually squashed into rock. Sandstone, limestone and chalk are all types of sedimentary rock, and they often contain fossils.

Metamorphic rocks

started out as igneous or sedimentary rocks, before being cooked at high temperatures by volcanic activity. The result of this sort of pressure cooking is to turn them into rock-hard metamorphic rock such as a slate, and to burn any fossil remains to a crisp.

Sedimentary rock cake

Because sedimentary rocks build up in layers (or strata) like cake, they are useful for dating fossils. Digging down through the layers is a bit like taking a journey back in time. On the top layer, you'll find remains of more recent animals and plants, but the further down you go, the older the fossils become.

The first palaeontologists realized that fossils found at the same layer almost certainly lived at the same time. This is how they worked out which dinosaurs lived with other dinosaurs. However, there is a flaw in this method – if the rock layers have been dug up or disturbed, it's possible to get completely the wrong date.

Nowadays, palaeontologists have moved on to an even more accurate way of dating dinosaurs. Each layer of rock contains a different amount of radio-activity, and palaeontologists now measure this radio-activity to work out when an animal lived and died. This time scale is accurate to within a few million years – this may sound a bit vague to you, but by geological standards, it's spot on.

Bone hunters

All this talk about rocks and radioactive dinosaur dating might make you worry that you need to be a genius to be a palaeontologist. But there's no need to think you'll never make the grade just because you're not making good grades at school.

While it's true that most professional dinosaur hunters have university degrees in geology or zoology, and use complicated modern technology, some discoveries have been made in surprizingly simple ways.

1. In the 1890s, John Bell Hatcher (a farmer turned bone hunter) got a little help to solve a big problem. He was looking for fossils of small mammals that lived alongside dinosaurs, and at the end of each day's work, all he'd have found were one or two fossilized

teeth. Then he had a brain-
wave that raised his next
day's catch to 87 teeth.

Hatcher had hatched
out a brilliant plan –
he let ants do the work
for him. The fossilized
teeth were exactly the
same size as the small
pieces of stone that ants heap
up on top of their nests. Hatcher simply dug up ant
hills and sifted through the soil to find the fossils.

2. Barnum Brown was an ace palaeontologist at the
turn of the 19th century. He liked wearing immacu-
late outfits and didn't like
digging in case he got them
dirty. For most people this
might be a problem, but it
didn't interfere with Brown's
uncanny knack for
discovering dinosaurs. The
secret to Brown's success was
that he followed his nose. It
was claimed that he could
smell dinosaurs, and it
certainly seemed to work.
Brown discovered several skeletons of T-rex,
Centrosaurus, Corythosaurus and Saurolophus
during his career.

3. Harley Garbani was born in 1920 and grew up on
a farm in California. At the age of eight he found a

fossilized camel bone, and was hooked on discovering dinosaurs from that day on. However, instead of being a trained palaeontologist, Garbani was a trained plumber. Nevertheless, he's one of the most successful dinosaur hunters ever. In 1966, he found the fossilized remains of the world's fourth-ever T-rex. Since then he's had no reason to pipe down, as he's found two more of them, while the rest of the world has only discovered eight other specimens altogether. When asked about the secret to his success, Garbini claims that he's "just a pretty lucky fella".

LOOK WHAT I FOUND IN THE GARDEN DEAR.

4. The clumsiness of Canadian palaeontologist Phil Currie gave him a head start in his search for dinosaurs. When he was on one expedition, he dropped his camera case down a hill. When he clambered down to retrieve it, he discovered that it had landed on the skull of a large dinosaur.

OUCH!

Dead dangerous discoveries

Discovering dinosaurs sounds like a great job, but it can be downright dangerous. On some expeditions, dinosaur hunters have almost become as extinct as the dinosaurs they were looking for. If you're thinking of setting off to find some fossilized remains, check out the dinosaur discoverer's do's and don't's.

Do – pack a medical kit. The dinosaur bug is not the only thing that has bitten palaeontologists. Rattlesnakes have often rattled dinosaur hunters in North America, while Professor Fraas's plan to study fossils in East Africa came to sticky end when he caught dysentery and was forced to run for home.

Do – watch out for other fossil hunters. In the early days of dinosaur discovery there was such a rush for remains that palaeontologists shot at their rivals and tried to steal fossils from each other.

Do – listen to advice. When young American dinosaur hunter Henry Osborn was on an 1880s expedition to Wyoming, he met a gold prospector who advised: "Young feller – either you'd better pull out the brim of your hat or pull in your nose." Luckily, Osborn listened. If he hadn't, he'd have suffered from an acute case of sunburn or even sunstroke. Dinosaur remains are nearly always found in tough terrain, and one of the most famous dinosaurs sites in the Badlands of Montana is so hot that it's called Hell Creek.

Do – look up often. Many palaeontologists have been so bowled over by their discoveries that they've also been bowled over by falling rocks.

Don't – dig unless you've got permission. In May 1992, 30 FBI agents raided the Black Hills Institute in South Dakota and impounded Sue, the world's largest T-rex. The reason for the raid was that the remains had been found inside a Sioux Indian Reservation and legally belonged to the Sioux.

Don't – get too carried away. On one occasion, a dozy dinosaur discoverer was so busy searching for dinosaur bones that he forgot to look where he was going, and fell down a cliff.

Don't – forget to check your transport. When Thomas Weston decided to search the canyons of the Red Deer River in the Canadian province of Alberta in 1888, he came up with the bright idea of building a large boat and making it into a floating headquarters. When it was finished, Weston loaded his team and equipment on board then set sail. Unfortunately, his plans were scuppered when the boat sprang a leak 13km down river. Having scrambled to the river bank, the waterlogged Weston could only sit and watch his expedition sinking without trace.

Dinosaur digging

Having survived the trip to the site and discovered some dinosaur bones, you'll probably want to start celebrating. But before you start tucking into the jelly and ice cream, you'll need to dig out the dinosaur. Over the years, dinosaur hunters have used a variety of equipment to unearth remains, but what do you think you'll need for a successful excavation?

A. Pneumatic drill
B. Bulldozer
C. Dentist's drill
D. Plaster of Paris
E. Dynamite
F. Chemical bath

Answer: A, C, D, F

A. Pneumatic drills are used to get through layers of tough rock. Palaeontologists must concentrate though, as one slip could easily destroy a fossil and their career along with it.

B. Using a bulldozer to dig up a dinosaur would make palaeontologists see red. However, bulldozers are sometimes used to help clear the area surrounding the dig. When a T-rex was found at Hell Creek in the United States, military engineers used bulldozers to build a road to the site. Articulated lorries were later used to remove the fossilized remains. Inventive palaeontologists have also taken advantage of all sorts of other transport, including camels, mules and even elephants, to move their finds.

C. The sound of a dentist's drill might give you nightmares, but it's sweet music to a palaeontologist's ears, as these are used back in the lab for working on small fossils. Dinosaur discoverers even use toothbrushes to give delicate remains a final polish, removing sand and silt.

D. Wrapping broken bones in plaster of Paris is the best way of keeping them together before transporting them from the site. This terrific technique was developed in 1877 by Othniel Marsh, after he watched doctors setting their patients' broken bones in plaster. It is still used today.

E. Using dynamite would probably see your dinosaur-discovering career going up in smoke, but in the early days some palaeontologists used it to blow the tops off hills. Unfortunately, this method had a major flaw – it destroyed the dinosaur bones along with the rocks!

F. You'd be dippy not to have a chemical bath back at the lab. Fossils can sometimes only be removed from rocks by bubbling chemicals.

Disappearing dinosaurs

After all the hard work that goes into uncovering dinosaurs, you might think that it would be hard for dinosaurs to disappear again – but you'd be wrong. Dinosaur remains have gone missing in curious circumstances around the world. Read the following newspaper cuttings and find out!

Fossil Fuel (1916)

Professor of Geology Miss Mignon Talbot admitted that she was "absolutely gutted" when she heard the news of the fire that had broken out at Mount Holyoke College's Geological Museum last night.

The fire not only completely destroyed the museum, it also destroyed one of its prize exhibits – the fossilized remains of a Podokesaurus. Professor Mignon had discovered the remains only five years earlier and had presented them to the museum for safekeeping.

Podokesaurus rises from the ashes

Like the legendary phoenix, it now seems that the lost dinosaur, Podokesaurus, is about to rise from the ashes of the disastrous fire that destroyed it a few months ago.

The dinosaur's discoverer, Professor Talbot, was given the

good news by curators at Yale University, who confirmed that they'd taken a cast of the dinosaur before it went up in smoke. As a result, Podokesaurus isn't lost to the world of palaeontology.

Dinosaurs destroyed (1944)

The sweet taste of success has turned to dust for German palaeontologist Ernst Stromer. During the 1920s and 30s, he turned back the sands of time as he dug through the Egyptian desert and discovered several new dinosaurs, including Aegyptosaurus and Bahariasaurus.

Herr Stromer brought them back for safekeeping in museums in Germany, but he hadn't counted on the arrival of World War II. Recent bombing raids have destroyed Stromer's finds and turned his dinosaur skeletons to dust.

NOW WE'RE DEADER THAN EVER!

Dinosaur detective

American dinosaur expert Professor Marsh has admitted that he enjoyed turning into a temporary private eye after finding the back half of an Anchisaurus skeleton in a Connecticut quarry.

Professor Marsh soon came up with an explanation for the disappearance of the front half of dinosaur. He realized that it had been shipped off from the quarry to be made into stone construction blocks.

"I was determined to leave no stone unturned in my search," the palaeontologist confirmed. He tracked the construction blocks

down to the site of a new bridge, but as the professor explained: "Unfortunately, I had arrived too late. The blocks containing the Anchisaurus remains were already in position. I couldn't get to them without demolishing the entire bridge, so the remains will have to stay in place until the bridge is due for replacement."

Footprints go walkabout (1996)

Australian police have confirmed that the world's only set of Stegosaurus footprints have gone walkabout.

The police confirmed that thieves had used power tools to drill the fossilized footprints out of the rocks Australian northwest, where they had lain for over 130 million years.

Top of the police's suspect list are

unscrupulous private collectors but there are very few clues to help them track the thieves down.

UH -OH!

Discover your own dinosaur

Luckily, it's very rare for dinosaurs to go missing. With a new species currently being discovered every six weeks, it's much more likely that even more dinosaurs will come to light in the near future.

There's even better news if you're worried that you may not be the lucky one. Many dinosaurs are discovered by ordinary people. After all, nearly half of Japan's dinosaur fossils have been found by students, while Seismosaurus was uncovered by a hiker, and all the dinosaurs in New Zealand were discovered by just one amateur palaeontologist – Joan Wiffen.

MUMMY!

Now you know what to look for, why not try making your very own dinosaur discovery. But even if you do strike it lucky, don't think that the hard work stops there...

DINOSAUR DETECTIVES

If there's one thing harder than discovering a dinosaur's remains, it's reconstructing what the animal looked like and how it lived. Imagine trying to put a jigsaw together without knowing what the finished puzzle should look like or even whether you've got all the pieces. That's the problem that most palaeontologists face, and it's one that only a great deal of detective work can solve.

Fake fossils
In the dirty, difficult conditions of a dinosaur dig, mistakes are dead easy to make. Over eager experts have been so keen to make a discovery that they've identified bird and crocodile bones, and even pieces of wood as belonging to dinosaurs. Using microscopes, the first bit of work for the dinosaur detective is to identify fake fossils and separate them from the real thing.

The overlooked dinosaur
The first remains of Compsognathus were unearthed in 1861, but it took several more years for them to be identified as belonging to a dinosaur. Compsognathus was a small meat-eating dinosaur, but its discoverer, Andrea Wagner, ignored what

he'd found because he thought that all dinosaurs were huge. It was almost ten years later when a different palaeontologist, Thomas Henry Huxley, recognized the remains to be those of a dinosaur.

A case of mistaken identity

Making a mistake over a few small fossils is one thing, but in 1923 an entire dinosaur was wrongly identified. Delighted to have found a new dinosaur, the palaeontologists called their find Gorgosaurus. It was a slimmer version of the two-legged Albertosaurus, with a smaller head. Unfortunately, it was later pointed out that the reason for these similarities was that Gorgosaurus was actually a young Albertosaurus – the dippy discoverers hadn't found a new type of dinosaur after all.

Rotten reconstructions

Finding a complete dinosaur skeleton is about as rare as seeing your head teacher smile, and trying to reconstruct what a dinosaur might have looked like from a muddle of bones has got some palaeontologists completely muddled. Palaeontologists study the skeletons of modern-day animal species to try to get clues, but it hasn't stopped them from coming up with some rotten reconstructions.

Sir Richard Owen's attempt to reconstruct a life-

sized Iguanodon was more a case of Iguano-*don't*
look like that. Owen's rotten reconstruction put
Iguanodon's thumb claw on its nose, and had the
dinosaur walking on four legs.

Palaeontologists might have smelled a rat when
they looked closely at Henry Osborn's first reconstruction of Tyrannosaurus rex. This early dinosaur
expert originally put the dinosaur's eye in its nasal
socket.

When one Apatosaurus skeleton was discovered, it
was almost complete except for its head. Nearby,
there happened to be the remains of a similar
sauropod called Camarasaurus, and the dinosaur
hunters simply added its head to the Apatosaurus.
It was over 75 years before this rotten reconstruction was discovered and every single Apatosaurus
skeleton was given some swift skull surgery.

Deinocheirus is one of the most fascinating and frustrating dinosaurs found so far. The only clue to its existence is an enormous pair of arms. Each arm is longer than a human being, and each hand has three claws that are longer than chopping knives. If they belonged to a meat-eating dinosaur, then the complete creature would have been unbelievably massive. But until any more remains are found, palaeontologists can only guess what Deinocheirus may have looked like.

Palaeontological puzzles

Having reconstructed dinosaurs, palaeontologists soon realized that this only created more detective work. Why don't you put your brain power to the test and see if you can track down the answers to these palaeontological puzzles?

1. Sauropod sizes
Puzzled palaeontologists have come up with some scatty suggestions to explain how the huge sauropods survived. Which of the following theories were actually published?

A. Sauropods were so heavy that they had to wade about getting support from deep water.

B. Their long necks were used as snorkels for breathing while in the water.

C. They had two brains.

2. Hadrosaur howlers

Scientists have made several howlers when trying to explain the reason for the elaborate crests of hadrosaurs. Which of the following theories is now accepted as the most likely?

A. They were the equivalent of a giant nose.

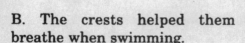

B. The crests helped them breathe when swimming.

C. They were used to signal to other dinosaurs.

3. Spiky solutions

What piece of modern technology led to a palaeontologist solving the mystery of Stegosaurus' spines?

A. A toaster

B. A car radiator

C. A computer

4. Transylvanian teaser

When an ankylosaur, a sauropod and a hadrosaur were discovered in Transylvania, they all had one thing in common – they were very small. Which is the most likely solution to this Transylvanian teaser?

A. They were all young dinosaurs.

B. They had lost touch with their bigger relatives.

C. Their fossilized remains had shrunk.

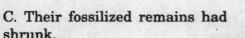

Answers:

1. All were published, but they have since been discredited.

A. This theory sank without trace when British scientist Kenneth Kermack proved that if sauropods were submerged, the water pressure on them would have crushed their lungs.

B. Sauropods used their long necks to reach plants high above the ground – not to breathe.

C. Although sauropods' heads only had room for a small brain, it was the only one they needed. The cavity at the base of their tail was a junction for nerves, not space for another brain.

2. C

To show that they gave a whole lot more than two hoots about this theory, a group of scientists built a replica model of a hydrosaur and put together computer models to simulate the sounds that the dinosaur might have made. When the palaeontologists published their findings, they even claimed that the dinosaur couldn't just play one note, but was capable of changing its pitch and phrase.

3. B

Explaining the purpose for the plates on the back of Stegosaurus was driving palaeontologists potty until 1976, when James Farlow came up with a stunning solution. He noticed that the plates looked like some parts of car radiators and concluded that overheated blood circulated in the plates until it cooled – the same way that a car radiator works.

4. B

Scientists put their brain power to good use when they suggested that Transylvania must have been an island during the Late Cretaceous period. The dinosaurs who were marooned there had stayed small as they had no competition from bigger relatives.

Dodgy deductions

The most exciting thing about coming home from a school trip is looking at your holiday snaps a few days later. It's a thrill that's shared by palaeontologists when they uncover a new dinosaur find.

However, while your pictures make perfect sense to you, they might be confusing to anyone finding them, say a few million years later.

Building up a complete picture from the "snapshots" provided by fossilized remains requires painstaking detective work, and some dinosaur deductions have been decidedly dodgy.

Sneaky footwork

In the 19th century, one dinosaur hunter in the American State of Texas found what he thought were human footprints in 100-million-year-old rocks. He concluded that this proved that humans and dinosaurs must have lived at the same time. However, his dodgy deduction was exposed when the footprints were studied more closely, and it was revealed that they were actually made by a two-legged dinosaur.

Egg on Andrew's face

Roy Chapman Andrews unearthed the first fossilized dinosaur eggs just after finding the remains of 14 adult Protoceratops. As a result, he assumed that the eggs contained baby Protoceratops. When he then found another dinosaur near the eggs, he thought that it must have been trying to eat them – so he called it Oviraptor philoceratops, meaning "egg thief who likes horned dinosaurs".

No one questioned Andrews' assumption until years later, when the eggs were examined and found to contain young Oviraptors. A find in 1995 revealed an Oviraptor that had died sitting on its nest of young. Although palaeontologists now think that Oviraptors were probably good mothers, their name and rotten reputation have stuck.

POLICE REPORT

The beasts of Bernissart

Sometimes even the best dinosaur detective work can't provide answers to a particular aspect of a dinosaur's life – or death. Why not join the palaeontology police and see if you can solve the mysterious case of the beasts of Bernissart.

Scene of incident: inside an ancient rock ravine at Bernissart, near Mons in Belgium.

Description of incident: coal miners discovered the grisly scene when they were working 300m below ground. When interviewed, they stated that they were cutting a new tunnel through the coal when they came across a jumble of bones. The bones weren't inside the coal deposits, but in a ravine. Having been called to the scene, dinosaur detectives have taken the bones from the mine for closer inspection.

Identification: the dinosaurs have all been identified as Iguanodon.

Number of dinosaurs: 31 complete skeletons have been found and reconstructed. Two kinds of Iguanodon were identified – presumably male and female – but there were no young dinosaurs.

Time of incident: approximately 100 million years ago.

Witnesses interviewed: none could be found alive.

Suspects:

Suspect A – predatory dinosaurs

A group of carnivores may have been working together to chase the herd of herbivorous Iguanodon. The predators may have been intending to trap their prey in the ravine so they could attack them more easily.

Suspect B – natural disaster

It's possible that the herd of Iguanodon were overtaken by a natural disaster such as a flood, and swept into the ravine to drown.

Suspect C – natural causes

The lack of young animals at the crime scene suggests that the ravine may have been some sort of dinosaur graveyard. All the Iguanodon found there were elderly beasts who went to the ravine to die.

The great dinosaur debate

You'd probably expect that as more clues are uncovered, the easier it would be to find out about dinosaurs. However, that's not the case in one of the greatest dinosaur debates of all time.

Trying to decide whether dinosaurs were cold-blooded like reptiles or warm-blooded like mammals has got palaeontologists extremely steamed up. Studies of reptiles such as lizards and mammals such as humans show that both kinds of animals live very differently.

REPTILES

COVERED IN SCALES.

SMALL BRAINS.

LEGS STICKING OUT OF THE SIDES OF THEIR BODIES.

REPTILES OFTEN LIVE IN COASTAL OR DESERT AREAS. THEY BASK IN THE SUN DURING THE DAY TO HEAT THEIR BLOOD AND REST AT NIGHT BECAUSE IT'S NOT WARM ENOUGH TO MOVE. THEY CAN BE EITHER SCAVENGERS, CARNIVORES OR HERBIVORES.

118

MAMMALS

BODIES COVERED IN FUR OR FAT TO RETAIN HEAT.

LARGE BRAINS.

MAMMALS MAINLY LIVE ON LAND. THEY ARE ACTIVE DURING THE DAY OR THE NIGHT.
THEY ARE EITHER **HERBIVORES** OR **PREDATORS**.

In the early days of palaeontology, everyone assumed that dinosaurs were cold-blooded, cumbersome and rather slow. They even named one specimen Morosaurus, meaning "stupid lizard".

DEAD AMAZING FACT

T-rex's brain was one of the largest in the history of life on earth, but so was its body. When compared to its size, its brain was actually quite small. Scientists have suggested that the dinosaur was about as intelligent as a bird, but that this was all the brain power T-rex needed to be massively successful.

After studying sauropods and other large dinosaurs, the first palaeontologists assumed that all dinosaurs were cold-blooded reptiles because:

SMALL-HEAD CONTAINING SMALL BRAIN - DOESN'T NEED CONSTANT ATTENTION

MASSIVE SIZE SOAKS UP MORE HEAT AND STAYS WARMER FOR LONGER.

HUGE BODY SO NEEDS LESS FOOD (ABOUT 10% OF AMOUNT REQUIRED BY WARM-BLOODED MAMMALS)

SLOW MOVING. DOESN'T NEED TO MOVE QUICKLY IF COLD BLOODED. BASKS IN SUN TO HEAT UP

DINOSAURS LAY EGGS AS REPTILES DO

But this view was challenged about 30 years ago with the discovery of a very different dinosaur. Stenonychosaurus was a two-legged carnivore with a large brain and very large eyes, whose remains suggested that dinosaurs may have been warm-blooded after all:

What do you think? Before making up your mind, the latest evidence may just swing the balance.

IF SAUROPODS WERE COLD-BLOODED THEY WOULD HAVE NEEDED HUGE HEARTS TO PUMP BLOOD AROUND THEIR HUGE BODIES TO SUPPLY THEIR HEAD, LUNGS AND OTHER ORGANS. BUT IF THEIR HEARTS WERE THE SAME DESIGN AS THOSE OF TODAY'S REPTILES, THEY COULDN'T HAVE DONE THIS WITHOUT DAMAGING THEIR LUNGS.

WELL, PERHAPS SAUROPODS' HEARTS WERE DIVIDED INTO TWO PARTS - ONE FOR THE LUNGS, AND THE OTHER FOR THE HEAD, BODY AND LEGS. IT'S SOMETHING FOUND IN MODERN-DAY MAMMALS.

YES, BUT ALL OF THEM ARE WARM-BLOODED. WHAT'S MORE, WE'VE ALSO DISCOVERED A MEAT-EATING DINOSAUR CALLED SYNTARSUS, WHOSE BONE CELLS AND BLOOD VESSELS ARE SIMILAR TO THOSE OF MODERN BIRDS AND MAMMALS.

At the moment it doesn't look as though the question will ever be absolutely proved one way or the other. One thing is certain though – palaeontologists will continue having heated arguments and giving each the cold shoulder over the issue for a long time to come.

But however many debates are held on this question, they're put in the shade by the greatest mystery of them all – what happened to the dinosaurs...

DISAPPEARING DINOSAURS

What happened next?

To find out what happened to the dinosaurs, let's go back in time 65 million years, to the end of the Cretaceous period...

It's a normal day on the fertile plains of North America. Huge herds of plant-eaters are keeping a careful eye out for attacks from predators. The sound of Parasaurolophus' hootings and Triceratops' massive munching fill the air.

In short, the dinosaurs are continuing to behave as they have done for millions of years. Of course, there have been changes during this time. Some species have died out, only to be replaced by animals that have evolved to be suited to different environments. But as the sun sets over the horizon, the dinosaurs settle down for the evening, confident that they are ideally suited to their environment and unaware of what is about to happen to them...

But what did happen to them?

For once, all scientists agree that something must have happened to end the dinosaurs' existence. For over 150 million years, the dinosaurs had proved themselves to be the most successful animals on the planet. Then they were wiped out by something big enough to cut down the huge herbivores, something that the swift and clever Stenonychosaurus couldn't outrun, something that even made mincemeat of Tyrannosaurus rex, the biggest, meanest dinosaur of them all.

What's more, while every single species of dinosaur was wiped out (along with many flying reptiles and sea-dwelling reptiles), other animals such as mammals, turtles and frogs survived.

Even stranger and harder to explain is the fact that sea crocodiles also became extinct, while their river-dwelling relatives survived.

This massive mystery has perplexed palaeontologists for years. And as you'd expect, they've come up with more than their fair share of totally barmy ideas to explain it...

CONSTIPATION IS THE CULPRIT. CHANGES IN VEGETATION CAUSED TOO MUCH STRAIN ON THEIR DIGESTIVE-SYSTEM.

 OH!

 IT'S ALL DOWN TO BORDEM, THEY'D ALL BEEN AROUND SO LONG THAT THEY JUST DIED OF IT.

 I'VE HAD ENOUGH OF THIS. FLUMP.

 NONSENSE, IT'S OBVIOUS THAT THEY WERE KILLED BY POISONOUS PLANTS.

 YUK!

 MY 'EGG-STINCTION' THEORY IS THE BEST. MAMMALS ATE ALL THEIR EGGS... OR ELSE A PLAGUE OF CATERPILLARS ATE ALL THE PLANTS.

 HOW DO YOU WANT IT, FRIED OR BOILED?

Prime suspect

If you're not convinced by any of these – and most
people aren't – palaeontologists have pointed the
finger at other possible culprits for the dinosaurs'
demise. Can you pick the current prime suspect
from the following line-up?

1. Volcanoes that blow their tops, overheating the
earth and hard-boiling all the dinosaurs' eggs.

2. An extra-terrestrial visitor crashing into earth.

3. Cooling of the climate, caused by the continents
moving.

4. Ultraviolet light, which caused blindness, the destruction of plants and deadly droughts.

Answer: 2
This idea is not as X-traordinary as it sounds. Many scientists think that the dinosaurs' extinction was caused by an asteroid crashing into the earth.

The solar system is a bit like a giant pinball machine, with small and large lumps of rock called asteroids whizzing through it. Every so often these rocks hit planets – with disastrous results.

A large asteroid hitting the earth would have spelt trouble with a capital T for the dinosaurs. Scientists have suggested that the impact could have been as much as 10,000 times greater than that made by detonating every nuclear bomb on earth today. In the first few hours, the dinosaurs would have faced:

1. Massively powerful earthquakes breaking open huge chasms in the earth's surface.
2. Huge tidal waves travelling around the world, covering the land and drowning anything in their path.
3. Strong gales fanning fires which spread to engulf trees and forests.

And that was just for starters...

Even if some dinosaurs survived these horrendous hazards, the worst horror of all was still waiting for them – a deadly dust cloud.

The force of the asteroid's impact would have created huge dust clouds that rose into the atmosphere. Within days, the sun would have darkened and would soon have been completely blotted out. For years, there would have been permanent night on earth. Without sunlight, plants would have withered away and died, along with the dinosaurs that ate them. As the herbivores died out, the carnivores' food supply would have disappeared too. Any cold-blooded animals would have gradually cooled down and, without the sun's warming rays, would have soon perished.

Proof at last

It's a great theory, isn't it? But until recently, it was only a theory. Up until about 20 years ago, there was a major hole in the idea – there was no proof that an enormous asteroid had ever hit our planet.

However, this all changed in June 1980, when

Professor Luis Alvarez and his son announced the results of years of research.

Scientists know that asteroids contain a metallic substance call iridium, which is only rarely found on earth. The dinosaur-mad duo showed that a thin layer of clay in the earth's crust dating from the time of the dinosaurs' extinction contains high amounts of iridium. Their explanation was that it must have come from an asteroid hitting the earth.

Some people still remained doubtful, though.

BUT IF EARTH WAS HIT BY A HUGE ASTEROID, WHERE'S THE CRATER?

A discovery in 1996 seemed to answer this question – a submerged crater more than 200km across was discovered off the coast of Mexico.

Convinced? Still unsure? Palaeontologists can only look for clues and suggest the most likely explanations. The bad news is that unless someone invents a time machine, we'll never know for certain what killed the dinosaurs. The good news is that this means that there are plenty of opportunities for palaeontologists to come up with their own awesome alternatives and occasional silly suggestions. One argument against this 'Impact theory' is that different dinosaurs took millions of years to become extinct. They didn't actually all die out at once.

And now for the even better news...

The death of the dinosaurs was even better news for the animals that remained on earth. Without the dinosaurs, the evolutionary road was suddenly open for new species to adapt, develop and eventually take over.

Stepping out from the giant shadows and the heavy footprints of the dinosaurs came the small shrew-like mammals. They had probably posed little threat during the dinosaurs' reign, and would have been easily overlooked by the huge animals. And yet, over millions and millions of years, this group of tiny mammals not only survived, but evolved into the creature that currently dominates life on earth – humankind.

131

EPILOGUE

How many species of dinosaur were there? Were they warm or cold-blooded? Why did the herbivore Pinacosaurus have two small holes in its skull above its nose? How did the dinosaurs die out?

No one knows the answers for sure, but these are just some of the questions that keep dinosaur detectives busy and drive palaeontologists potty. Puzzles like these also look certain to ensure that while the dinosaurs became extinct millions of years ago, they are refusing to roll over and die. In fact, they are still hitting the headlines daily.

Suchomimus – such a huge catch
An 11m skeleton has revealed an entirely new predator which lived in Africa 100 million years ago. Suchomimus' sharp cone-shaped teeth are ideal for piercing slippery prey, leading palaeontologists to deduce that it was a fish-eating predator.

T-rex fetches a monster price
The largest T-rex ever discovered has recently been sold at a monster price. At an auction in New York, the Chicago Field Museum of Natural History paid a record $8.4 million (£5 million) for the remains.

Titanosaurus babies

A nesting site containing Titanosaurus eggs has been discovered in South America. Covering around 2·5 square km, the vast site contains hundreds of eggs laid by this relative of Apatosaurus. Palaeontologists have discovered that the embryos inside the eggs have bones, teeth and fossilized skin.

When dinosaurs were first discovered, scientists assumed that they were clumsy and stupid, but we now know that they were the most successful creatures that ever lived on earth. Each new discovery reveals another dead amazing aspect of the dinosaurs' way of life, and it's certain that new finds will lead to new theories.

We may even learn something from the dinosaurs' success – and even, perhaps, from their downfall. If not, in a few million years, it may not be dead dinosaurs that are being studied, but a whole new set of fossilized remains!

The Knowledge

The Gobsmacking Galaxy

Awful Art

Mind-blowing Music

Groovy Movies

Smashin' Fashion

Mind-boggling Buildings

Spoilt Royals

Potty Politics

Crashing Computers

Flaming Olympics

Dreadful Drama

Triffic Chocolate

Awesome Archaeology

Spectacular Special Effects

HORRIBLE SCIENCE

Ugly Bugs
Blood, Bones and Body Bits
Nasty Nature
Chemical Chaos
Fatal Forces
Sounds Dreadful
Disgusting Digestion
Evolve or Die
Vicious Veg
Bulging Brains
Frightening Light
Shocking Electricity
Deadly Diseases
Microscopic Monsters
Killer Energy
The Body Owner's Handbook

Horrible Science Specials:
Suffering Scientists
Explosive Experiments

Also available:
The Awfully Big Quiz Book

Two books in one:
Ugly Bugs and Nasty Nature
Blood, Bones and Body Bits and Chemical Chaos
Bulging Brains and Disgusting Digestion
Frightening Light and Sounds Dreadful

Science has never been so horrible!